DATE DUE

NO 08			
NO 20			

The Christian Scientists (The
American Religious
Jean Kinney Williams
AR B.L.: 9.2
Points: 3.0

THE CHRISTIAN SCIENTISTS

THE CHRISTIAN SCIENTISTS

JEAN KINNEY WILLIAMS

American Religious Experience

Franklin Watts
A Division of Grolier Publishing
New York / London / Hong Kong / Sydney
Danbury, Connecticut

Interior design by Molly Heron
Photos ©: AP/Wide World Photos: 84; Archive Photos: 8, 64, 92; Brown Brothers: 11, 18, 34, 37, 38, 44, 48, 52, 53, 74, 76; Corbis-Bettmann: 14, 20, 23, 26, 31, 32, 63, 66, 71; Culver Pictures: 35; UPI/Corbis-Bettmann: 79; Photo Researchers: cover (Spencer Grant).

Library of Congress Cataloging-in-Publication Data

Williams, Jean Kinney.
The Christian Scientists / by Jean Kinney Williams.

p.   cm. — (American religious experience)
Summary: Provides a history of Christian Scientists, covering their doctrines and practices, organization, place in American society, and changes in beliefs, as well as discussing the work of Mary Baker Eddy.
ISBN 0-531-11309-4
1. Christian Science—United States—History—Juvenile literature. 2. United States—Church history—Juvenile literature. 4. Christian Scientists—United States—Juvenile literature.
5. Christian Science.   [1. Eddy Mary Baker, 1821–1910.]
I. Title. II. Series.
BX6931.W55   1996   96–9878
   289.5—dc20   CIP
                                                                                AC

CONTENTS

THE CHRISTIAN SCIENTISTS

WHO ARE THE CHRISTIAN SCIENTISTS?

On February 1, 1866, in the factory town of Lynn, Massachusetts, a middle-aged woman struggled across the icy lanes toward an evening meeting of a local civic group. To those who knew of her, she might have been considered a rather pitiful figure. Twenty-two years earlier, her first husband had died after just six months of marriage. She gave birth to his child a few months later, but due to her poor health, which had plagued her from childhood, and the hardship she faced as a result of her husband's death, she had to give up care of her son to a foster family.

Mary Baker Eddy (she dropped the name of her first husband when she married Asa Eddy in 1877) had more than her share of challenges. An older brother to whom she'd been very close, and who seemed to have a brilliant career ahead of him in New England politics, also died prematurely. Because of her lifelong poor health, she often sought out the latest health fad or cure. After the death of her first husband, George Glover, her status as a single woman had left her dependent on family members. And her second husband, Daniel Patterson, proved unstable and unfaithful. Nevertheless, she was deeply religious and always sure of God's love for her, despite her difficult life.

That winter evening in 1866, Mary felt well enough to go out for the evening. But her physical well-being suffered another setback when she slipped on the ice, injured her head, and, during the next couple of days, thought herself to be near death.

Nineteenth-century medicine and health fads had made little impact on her illnesses over the years; as she lay in bed with her head injury, she turned to the Bible, which she read regularly. As she pondered an account in the Gospel of Matthew of a healing performed by Jesus of Nazareth, she seemed to experience a similar healing—immediate and instantaneous. Not only that, but the healing of her head injury, she said, included a momentary vision of God's spiritual world. From that vision came a movement that would cause quite a stir in the state of Christianity of her day, already turned upside down by a variety of new religions and scientific theories and discoveries. Mary Baker Eddy, as she became known to the world after her remarriage in 1877, would live to be nearly ninety and achieve fame around the world as the "discoverer" of Christian Science.

Some people might know of the church for its members' reliance on God for healing rather than on conventional medical treatment; perhaps you've noticed a Christian Science Reading Room on a busy downtown street, or the *Christian Science Monitor* newspaper in the library or on newsstands.

But Christian Scientists will tell you that there is much more to their church than avoiding traditional medical care. They are encouraged to live their faith daily by relying completely on God for

Mary Baker Eddy in 1886

help in every need, including education, careers, or relationships. That means a new way of looking at reality. Eddy and those who followed her attempted to demonstrate this reality, just as one would try to demonstrate any scientific principle. "Divine Principle," in fact, was one term Eddy used to describe the set of spiritual rules she claimed to encounter in her healing vision.

Science played a great part in nineteenth-century life for Americans and Europeans. Inventions such as the steam locomotive and the telegraph brought people closer together in the vast United States. Charles Darwin, after observing wildlife and studying fossils from the Galapagos Islands and South America, presented the scientific theory that all living beings in existence had evolved and were selected by nature for survival, as opposed to the belief that God made all living creatures just as they are today. Such discoveries and theories were changing the way people thought about all of life.

One effect that science had on intellectual life in the ever-changing nineteenth century was that new ideas needed to be proven. That was just what Mary Baker Eddy set out to do. She began with a few students, and then developed a fledgling healing practice in which she paired up with one of her earliest pupils.

It was almost ten years after her accident and healing that Eddy published her ideas in the book *Science and Health*, later adding *with Key to the Scriptures* to its title, the key being a glossary and interpretation of biblical terms. The book explained her discovery that matter was not real, and that in spite of the appearance of the human body, we are not made up of matter, either. Because God is purely spiritual, and people are said in the Bible to be made in God's image, then we also are purely spiritual, she taught.

The unreality of matter was a theory already put forth by a religious movement called Transcendentalism, which in turn had borrowed it from Asian religions. But Eddy felt she could prove the unreality of matter *and* the existence of God at the same time. The easiest and most noticeable way for her to demonstrate her Christian Science was through healing. By focusing on the perfection of humans as existing in God's image, she began performing what seemed to be miraculous healings. With a group of her students she formed a church in Boston in 1879—the Church of Christ, Scientist. The name of the church carried two messages: the church was a Christian one, based on the teachings of Jesus of Nazareth; the word "Scientist" implied authority and knowledge, based on proven facts.

Eddy's church certainly seemed remarkable to people at the time. But her discovery, as she called it, came about at a time when people were making all kinds of spiritual and healing claims. Several years earlier, she had been a patient of a "mind-curer" named Phineas P. Quimby, who said he healed people by helping them get rid of false ideas about religion or illness. Quimby and others used mesmerism, a type of hypnotism, in their practices. Mesmerists traveled around the country putting on "performances." One group, the Spiritualists, held seances in which they said they communicated with the dead. But Eddy wrote, "I never could believe in Spiritualism." She did not consider her work a branch of Spiritualism at all.

Though Eddy considered her theories to be strictly Christian and based on the Bible, many saw Christian Science as just another "far out" group. Ministers of traditional churches warned their congregations about it. Her role as pastor of a church was unusual for her time; women still could not vote in the United States, and they

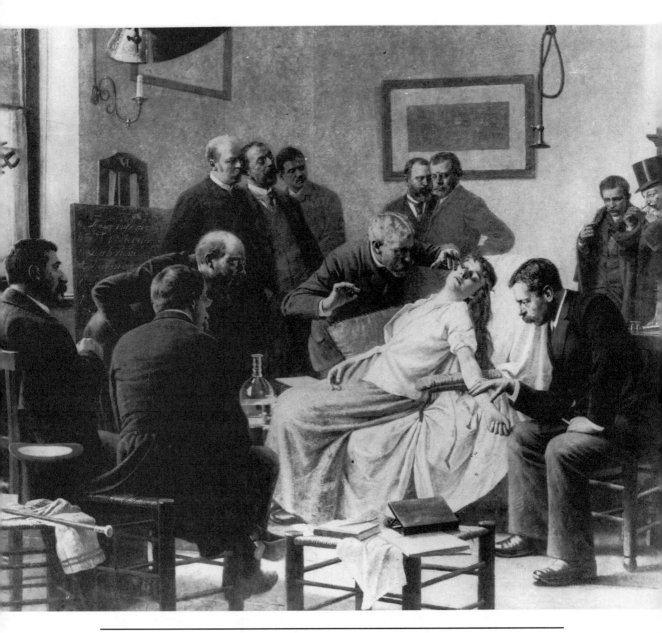

There was much interest in the link between psychology and medicine in the nineteenth century, as seen in this painting, An Experiment in Hypnotism.

seldom held such authoritative positions. Many men, unwilling to give her ideas serious consideration, simply ridiculed her.

But slowly the church grew. It continued to expand after Eddy's death in 1910, spreading to Europe and other parts of the world. Its early membership, formed from working-class citizens in search of healing, soon included physicians, politicians, and successful business people from all over the country and beyond.

There is no clergy in the Christian Science church. Congregations elect readers who read selections from the Bible and *Science and Health* each Sunday. Specially trained Christian Science healers, known as practitioners, work full-time at healing and have offices and treat patients much like physicians.

Christian Scientists celebrated the seventy-fifth anniversary of *Science and Health* at their annual church meeting in 1950. Scientists were told that, for the forty-eighth year in a row, membership had grown more each year than the gain of 2,784 members reported in 1902. Though member figures are not released publicly, church observers estimated the mid-century membership to be as high as 325,000. By the time Christian Scientists marked their hundredth anniversary in 1979, though, a decline was in place, and membership was estimated to be down by about 100,000.

Today the Church of Christ, Scientist is in a state of transition. At the end of the nineteenth century, Eddy predicted that Christian Science would, within fifty years, become "the dominant religious belief of the world."[1] Many of its churches have closed, however, in the United States and around the world, although it is growing in some areas. In recent years, Christian Science parents whose children died when traditional medical treatment was refused have narrowly avoided being convicted when their cases were overturned by the

Supreme Court. Church leaders invested and lost tens of millions of dollars in cable-television ventures in the early 1990s, which led to protests by church members across the country.

Where is the Christian Science church heading? Thousands of healing testimonies that have been published by the church for more than a century indicate a form of Christianity with much to offer society. Christian Science church branches have reading rooms stocked with church literature. These rooms are open to the public, but fewer people have used them in recent years.

How the story of the Church of Christ, Scientist began, though, is quite clear. It began with a New England woman, Mary Baker Eddy, who was not quite as simple as she appeared.

MARY BAKER'S LIFE OF PAIN

By 1821, the story of the Pilgrims' landing at Plymouth Rock in Massachusetts was two centuries old. Their religion, though, remained a leading social force in New England, which still was the heart of the United States of America.

The American Revolution, with its flags and battles, had occurred thirty-five years earlier. But a quieter revolution was taking place in America in the early 1800s. Some citizens, given the freedom to practice religion as they saw fit, began rejecting the mainstream religion of the day in search of something different. In that same year, 1821, a young man named Ralph Waldo Emerson graduated from Harvard University; he would soon add many new ideas to America's religious forum.

Mary Baker was born that year, the sixth and last child of Mark and Abigail Baker of Bow, New Hampshire. Her father, a farmer, was steeped in stern New England Puritanism, while Abigail, as Mary later described her, was a warm and loving mother. Mary was close

A drawing of Mary Baker Eddy's birthplace in Bow, New Hampshire

to her older sisters and brothers. Letters between family members showed concern about Mary, who seemed to have more than the usual share of fevers and colds.

Her older brothers broke away from the farm life that Mark Baker envisioned for his sons. One brother, Albert, studied law, and he encouraged Mary to further her own studies. Her education was erratic, depending on her health, but she seemed especially to enjoy poetry. She wrote many poems throughout her life; as an adult leading her own church, her poetry took the form of hymns that are still sung today.

Young Mary was concerned about her health, too. When she was twelve years old, she wrote a lengthy poem about the tie between spiritual health and physical health. By the time she was in her teens, she was trying the "Graham diet," named after Sylvester Graham. He believed that food other than coarse bread, vegetables, and water was too rich for the body. (Graham flour and graham crackers are also named after him.) Through a cousin's influence, she tried homeopathic medicine, based on the belief that certain drugs, if taken in large doses would worsen symptoms of a disease, but if taken in small doses would actually cure the disease.

She was also a thoughtful girl, and began forming her own ideas about God early on. She and her father had many disagreements over religion, especially on the subject of predestination. The Bakers' Congregational church taught the notion that only some people in the world are destined to be saved by God. The teachings of John Calvin, a religious reformer in Switzerland in the 1500s, about predestination and salvation by God's grace alone, had greatly influenced the Puritans.

Mary never believed that a good and loving God would select

only a certain group of people to live eternally in Heaven, and sometimes her arguments with her father over this would leave her physically ill. The Bakers moved when Mary was a teenager and joined a different Congregational church, whose minister insisted that Mary, too, profess to believe in predestination. This could have been an emotional struggle for Mary, and she became ill for a while, but she did join the church.

By the 1830s, there were other young women who began to doubt their Calvinist religious upbringing. The abolitionist Lucy Colman, for example, did not believe a loving God would permit slavery. Reformers in later years, such as Elizabeth Cady Stanton, helped lead campaigns for women's rights.

Also in the 1830s, a philosophy called Transcendentalism, with Ralph Waldo Emerson as one of its leaders, was finding more followers. Emerson published his book *Nature* in 1836, saying, "Behind . . . fact or material appearance . . . lay the spiritual reality [of] higher laws, unimagined potentialities."[1] Mainstream Christianity taught that revelations and miracles were in the past; but Emerson spoke of new revelations, something orthodox Christianity didn't think possible. The Unitarian church was a growing spiritual movement in New England at the time, and some members tried to integrate spiritual ideas such as Emerson's into their doctrine.

Mary Baker enjoyed keeping up with changing ideas in society,

Ralph Waldo Emerson, like Mary Baker Eddy, pondered the reality of the physical world and helped begin a movement called Transcendentalism.

but her health suffered as she went through personal losses such as the death of her much-loved brother Albert in 1841. Some of the poetry she wrote was printed in local newspapers. In one poem, she wondered if she, too, would succumb to an early death. Mary's happy marriage to George Glover in 1843 lasted only half a year before he suddenly died. Their son, George, was born just a few months later, but Mary's health left her unable to care for him or herself for several months.

She spent the next several years battling illness and frustrations: her son was unruly, she was unsure of herself as a mother, and she was still dependent on her family. The Congregational church she attended did not offer the comfort she sought, and doctors could do little for her. She attended a lecture on phrenology, which suggested that mental and physical health were related. This made sense to Mary, who noticed how her own health was affected by the circumstances in her life. Another movement gaining attention was Spiritualism, which said that communication with the dead was possible through scientific laws; they compared the process to that of the newly invented telegraph. For many Americans leaving behind mainstream Protestantism, Spiritualism even served as a religion. But Mary never took Spiritualism seriously, and later she encountered many Spiritualists as she worked to establish her own church. She

Members of the movement called Spiritualism claimed to be in touch with the spirits of those who had died. Many demonstrations of Spiritualism, such as the one in this picture, turned out to be hoaxes.

included a chapter exposing the errors of spiritualist practice in her book, *Science and Health*.

In the meantime, Mary's son came between her and other family members on whom she depended. Her father, Mark Baker, who was the boy's legal guardian, wanted Mary to give up George. Mary's married sister Abigail Tilton offered her a home, but without her son. George finally went to live with the woman who'd cared for him since his infancy. Shortly after this, Mary's mother Abigail died; her father remarried within a year, and Mary moved in with her sister Abigail. But in her despondency over losing her son and her mother, Mary became very ill. She was weak and complained of a spinal illness.

Mary kept her mind and pen occupied with poetry, and she was an avid reader, keeping up with current events. One national debate gaining more attention was that of slavery; Sibyl Wilbur, a biographer of Mary Baker Eddy, related Mary's statement, at a party being given by her socially prominent sister, that "the South as well as the North suffers from the continuance of slavery and its spread to other states." This was a controversial opinion spoken at a time when women were not supposed to voice them. "I dare to speak what I believe in any house," Mary calmly replied to her sister's reprimand.[2] Mary remained a daily Bible reader, and in her poetry, she touched on topics such as women's rights and the apparent coming of a civil war. Sometimes her poetry spoke of personal longings, such as a wish to see her mother again.

In 1853, Mary married her dentist, Daniel Patterson, but on their wedding day, in her father's home, she was too ill to come downstairs herself. Patterson carried her down to take their wedding vows, then carried her back up immediately afterward. She remained bed-ridden off and on for several years as her husband made a meager living in dentistry; Mary turned away from traditional doctors as she took more and more interest in homeopathy. Complaining mostly of nervous disorders, she also sought out various health fads, some of which could provide temporary help, but no cures. A visit to a "water cure" institute, for example, left her feeling worse.

By the early 1860s, Phineas P. Quimby, from Portland, Maine, was becoming widely known as a healer for his "mind-cures." He had studied mesmerism, named for its Viennese physician-founder, Franz Anton Mesmer, who claimed to harness the powers of an unseen magnetic "fluid" produced by the human body. Quimby became convinced that he could perform mental healing on patients, and that most illnesses were psychosomatic, or originating in the mind. He claimed to be clairvoyant, or a mind-reader, and said he "took the feelings of my patient . . . feeling their aches and pains."[3]

When Mary arrived in Portland in 1862 to undergo yet another type of healing, she was forty-one years old and desperate; she was not in good health, and her husband was in a Confederate prison, having strayed too close to enemy lines while on a government mission for the Union in the Civil War. In Quimby she found a man who listened closely to his patients and sympathized with their plight. Though he considered himself a follower of Jesus, he believed most of his patients' problems were caused by fear planted in their minds by doctors, and by inner conflicts caused by organized religion.

Mary began responding to Quimby's treatments and she, too, spread the word of his services. She sent a poem and article about him to the local newspaper and defended him against charges that he was a Spiritualist. She claimed, rather, that Quimby had "superior wisdom," and she even stayed in Portland for three months to observe his healing methods.[4]

Phineas Parkhurst Quimby was an untrained healer working in Maine who became famous for his "mind-cures." He believed that people's illnesses were caused by their fears of disease, or by inner conflicts. Mary Baker Eddy became his patient in the mid-1860s.

Her husband, who had escaped from prison, joined her in Maine, and they returned to New Hampshire by the end of 1862. Her illnesses, such as severe headaches, also returned, and she headed back to Portland. She continued to study Quimby's methods, and even lectured on them. Quimby's ideas sparked something in her, and Mary began to believe that the science of healing could be combined with a loving Christian faith. In studying homeopathy and Quimby's healing methods, she also began to see illnesses as more mental than physical.

In 1864, Mary was visiting a friend who was a zealous Spiritualist. While there, she seemed to fall into two "trances," serving as a medium for her brother Albert to speak through. Her critics pointed to such episodes to suggest that she was more into cults than Christianity. But she claimed rather that she had faked the trances in order to show that one who did not believe in Spiritualism could reproduce such states. Her description of the event indicates how determined she was to find her own path toward well-being, rather than follow someone else's methods.

At this point, Mary's life seemed a mess: her health was precarious, and her husband was being unfaithful to her. The next year, in 1865, her father died. Still corresponding with Quimby and feeling somewhat dependent on him, she learned of his death, too, in early 1866. Little did she know that a turning point was near, after which her life would take on a new direction.

HEALING
THE SICK

Jn what seemed to be Mary Patterson's darkest days—she was separated from her second husband, she was only occasionally healthy enough to work as a teacher, she had lost much of her family, and she was estranged from her only child—her optimism remained high. She especially never gave up on turning to God for answers, even after so many difficult and disappointing experiences.

When her fall on the ice in 1866 left her bedridden again, she looked once more to God for the meaning of her life. At last she believed her lifelong questions were being answered.

Mary Patterson was living in Lynn, Massachusetts, a small shoe-factory town. The evening of her fall, she was on her way to a temperance meeting, where people discussed ways to discourage, or even prohibit, the drinking of alcohol. It was the first year after the end of the American Civil War, and many abolitionists, having succeeded in their antislavery cause, turned their attention to other issues, such as temperance movements and women's rights.

Having survived the devastating Civil War, the country was looking west, and railroads were carrying settlers away from crowded Eastern cities. For the most part, America's Puritan heritage was giving way to a new era. Progress wasn't measured in spiritual terms anymore, but in material gain. Men got rich in the making of towns and cities that sprang up across the prairies and mountains, all the way to California. Ministers saw their church congregations more easily distracted now by other, less demanding religions and by scientific theories such as Charles Darwin's ideas on evolution, which he first published in 1859. Wednesday evening church services—which had been a tradition, along with Sunday services, among the American mainstream Christian churches—had fewer and fewer attendants.

It seemed the Puritans were becoming a relic of the past, but Mary still found much to admire in them, in spite of the differences she had with their Calvinist Christianity. She appreciated the God-fearing ways of people like her mother and father, and she still practiced the daily habits of prayer and Scripture reading she'd learned at home.

So when Mary lay in bed after her fall on the ice and saw little hope in the faces of those caring for her, she opened her Bible. In Matthew's Gospel she read an account of Jesus healing a man with a lifelong disability.

Robert Peel, a twentieth-century Christian Scientist who wrote a three-volume biography of Mary Baker Eddy, said that as she pondered one of Jesus' many healings, she was given a vision and "saw all being as spiritual, divine, immortal, wholly good. There was no room for fear or pain or death, no room for the limits that men define as matter."[1] From that moment on, she put herself totally in God's care, rather than depending on a doctor or other healer. And

Temperance movements, which sought to restrict or eliminate alcohol consumption among the public, were everywhere after the Civil War. Mary Baker Eddy was on her way to a temperance meeting in February 1866 when she injured her head by slipping on an icy path. She claimed to be healed a few days later by what she later called "Christian Science."

her injury was healed. Christian Scientists consider this point in Eddy's life the beginning of a faith that would spread to thousands of others who would also experience similar healings.

Though she'd lived a sickly forty-five years, she would live her next forty-five years vigorously. None of these years would be easy, but now she had her purpose: to relate her joyful, yet pragmatic, vision of God, and to teach others about the reality of life. This reality, she said, focused on the spiritual rather than on matter or the physical world. It would be a while, though, before she was ready to lead a new movement into public view; this was a time when women as religious leaders were not so uncommon, but still struggling with opposition from traditional religion.

Her "spinal affection," as she called it, flared up again, and her marriage to Daniel Patterson finally ended in August 1866. During the next three years, she went from one boarding house to another in various Massachusetts towns, working occasionally as a teacher and reading the Bible. She concluded that the healing of her head injury had not been miraculous, but rather a natural part of God's spiritual world. She taught her ideas to anyone who would listen. Sometimes the Spiritualists were the most receptive listeners, even though Mary had dismissed their ideas.

She also was credited with many healings in this period of her life, including that of her sister Martha's daughter, and another

---

Jesus of Nazareth was not divine, Mrs. Eddy taught Christian Scientists, but he was the first Christian Scientist. With constant striving and learning, all could heal as Jesus did, she believed.

woman who was thought to be near death in childbirth. But Mrs. Glover, as Mary began referring to herself again, would find that her new religion eventually would come between her and her remaining family members. As one biographer put it, "the acceptance of Mrs. Glover's teachings would lead to a complete revolution of thought, [and] they began to draw away from her."[2]

Mary Glover's teaching on the unreality of matter wasn't new; the Transcendentalists had pondered the same idea. But she made it the center of her teaching, and to accept her ideas, one had to look at the Bible and life in a whole new light. For many, this was not easy. Some people just didn't agree, for example, with her strong conviction that all illnesses, as part of the unreal world of matter, were thus not real. But she was sure enough of her vision, especially after performing several healings, that she advertised in a Boston Spiritualist newspaper for students in 1868:[3]

> ANY PERSON desiring to learn how to heal the sick can receive of the undersigned instruction that will enable them to commence healing on a principle of science with a success far beyond any of the present modes. No medicine, electricity, physiology or hygiene required for unparalleled success in the most difficult cases. No pay is required unless this skill is obtained. Address, MRS. MARY B. GLOVER, Amesbury, Mass., Box 61   tf†—June 20.

For a few years after her fall on the ice and discovery of Christian Science, Mrs. Eddy lived in various homes in Massachusetts. She stayed here, at the Amesbury home of Captain and Mrs. Nathaniel Webster, in 1866 and 1867.

In 1870, she returned to Lynn with a promising student, Richard Kennedy. He would practice as a healer, while Mrs. Glover would teach and work on writing down her theories. Like Quimby, she referred to her ideas on healing as "Science." Many of her students came to her after being healed in Kennedy's office. Her life of poverty began to change as she was able to charge a regular fee for classes. Her students were mostly shoe factory workers from Lynn, attending classes in her rented rooms; for now, it was progress enough.

The once sickly Mrs. Glover grew into a strong and dynamic teacher who demanded much of her students, and with her clear ideas of what she called "Science," she often was described as having a presence that filled a room, despite her slender stature. She was considered attractive and much younger looking than her age. People often commented on her deep-set eyes. One student described her this way: "Her most prominent feature were the eyes, dark blue with a wonderful lustre, but sad, very sad at times, yet with a glory shining through. . . . I should say she was naturally joy-loving and light-hearted, but the desertion of her friends and relatives had saddened her."[4]

She had much to teach her students, but they sometimes confused her teachings, which she considered strictly Christian, with

---

During the years of her religious leadership, people often commented on Mary Baker Eddy's appearance, especially her eyes. Many of her students referred to her as "Mother."

After she began teaching classes in Christian Science, Mrs. Eddy was able to buy her own home in Lynn, Massachusetts, where she finished her text, Science and Health.

other health or religious fads of the day, such as mesmerism or Spiritualism. Jesus, she taught them, was not divine but was a Scientist. Though Christ's Apostles also practiced it, the art of healing was lost over the years by Christian churches. She asserted that healing is a natural part of God's world, and not something for which people can take credit. Though the conquering of sin and the material senses was the main theme in Christian Science, healing of physical illnesses was what attracted the most attention.

A misunderstanding of her doctrine on the part of her students could bring a sharp rebuke from Eddy, one side of her personality that would draw criticism and often cause tension in the new movement. She always claimed, though, to be correcting the wrong idea, not the person, and many of her students became quite attached to her. Her more successful students, like Richard Kennedy, went on to set up their own practices.

Before long, she discovered how strong a leader the Christian Science movement needed. Some of her students, once they were practicing as healers, began to compete against each other. They envied one another's successes or became jealous of Mary's attention toward certain students.

One student who turned against Mrs. Glover and her teachings was Wallace Wright. He wrote a letter to the Lynn newspaper, calling Christian Science a threat to Christian families and challenging Mary to explain the nonreality of visible conditions such as tumors or broken bones. He also charged that she merely practiced a type of mesmerism. Richard Kennedy had included the touching of patients, such as rubbing his hands on their heads, as a part of his healings, and Mary began to consider that unwise because of its similarity to mesmerism. When she discouraged Kennedy from touching any more patients, their partnership became uneasy; by 1872, they no longer worked together.

To the public, Kennedy was still associated with Christian Science, though he didn't practice healing the way Mrs. Glover would have wanted. She began to call him a mesmerist. Through Kennedy's use of touch, she believed, he made patients dependent on him, rather than on God and prayer.

With that in mind, Mary quit teaching regularly from 1872 to

1875 to work on a textbook that would explain her theories. She also supervised her students as they set up their own healing practices. She took the opportunity in her book to speak out against mesmerists, and in a letter in 1872, she had called Richard Kennedy a "wicked boy."[5] Nevertheless, Mary always remembered these early days of her movement, when she was able to know her students personally, as a happy time.

As she worked on her book, Mrs. Glover maintained her healing practice, and eventually she began to conduct services in a rented hall. She also spent much time writing to former students who had their own practices. She answered their pleas for help by reminding and encouraging them to bring their problems first to God, or "divine Principle." Having moved from boarding houses to rented rooms repeatedly over the years, she was finally able, after a few years of steady working, to buy herself a small house. Even then, she had to rent out all but two of the rooms. When she finished her book, she "waited patiently for six weeks" for God to tell her its title, and the words *Science and Health* came to her one night.[6] Some of her students helped pay for its publication, which was delayed because of several printing errors. Sales were slow at first. But she always considered it her greatest achievement.

MARY BAKER EDDY GAINS A FOLLOWING

4

*T*hough Christian Scientists don't consider Mary Baker Eddy divine, she is seen as someone having a key role in bringing about God's kingdom as it is supposed to be. Her writings are considered divinely inspired. The walls of Christian Science churches, such as the beautiful Mother Church, called the First Church of Christ, Scientist, display inscriptions from the Bible as well as her book, *Science and Health*.

Robert Peel wrote in his three-volume biography of Mary Baker Eddy, "For a woman to preach, lecture, write for newspapers, challenge the doctors and the clergy, claim a new religious revelation and a new scientific discovery . . . was in itself enough to make her an object of suspicion to cautious Yankees."[1] Some criticized her for revising her book so often: Because she claimed it was divinely inspired, they asked, couldn't God get it right the first time? But she was always searching for the right words to express her visions of spiritual reality, which she claimed to understand better as the years went by. Shortly before her death, she said to a student, "I feel I am just beginning to understand Science and Health."[2]

In the preface to *Science and Health,* she wrote, "The time for thinkers has come," and she gave readers plenty to think about. She quoted the Bible often, and referred to God as "our Father-Mother God." God also was described by the terms Life, Love, Spirit, Principle, Soul, Truth, and Mind. The phrase "mortal mind" described the human tendency to see only physical realities, the root of all error.

Science and Health tells readers that each person is an individual and unique "idea" of divine Mind, not a physical body, and angels are "God's thoughts passing to man."[3] Sickness, sin, and evil are not a part of God's world, and therefore are not real. To think they are real is an error. In prayer, visualize the perfect image of a person as made by God, and the sin or sickness that seems to be real can vanish. "Remove error from thought, and it will not appear in effect," she told readers.[4] This is the healing principle Mary demonstrated first to herself and then to others.

Jesus of Nazareth was not a divine being, according to Eddy, but by his healings and by overcoming death he shows us what is possible through divine Science. She thus referred to him as the "Master." In her glossary (which she added later to the book) she describes Jesus as "the highest human corporeal concept of the divine idea, rebuking and destroying error and bringing to light man's immortality."[5] Hell is not real, but is the "evil beliefs which originates in mortals,"[6] and "[t]he sinner makes his own hell by doing evil."[7]

In her earlier editions, she had much to say about something she called "malicious animal magnetism," thought of as a form of mesmerism. Though she wrote that evil is not a power unto itself (there's no such thing as the devil, for example), she credited animal magnetism or mesmerism for all of the trouble in her Christian Science movement. Those who had turned against her would think evil thoughts about her or other Christian Science leaders, and illnesses or personality conflicts would result, she said. Though later editions of *Science and Health* and other Christian Science publications contained very little about malicious animal magnetism, her recognition of it remained an important part of her teachings and daily life (she even tried to sue a former student for using it), and it was another aspect of Christian Science that some critics would point to as being absurd.

In spite of the critics, her movement continued to carry on after the publication of her book. Many of her early students came to her for healing, often from Spiritualist groups. One man who sought her out for healing and then became a student and practitioner, Asa Gilbert Eddy, revived Mary one day when she had what she called a violent seizure. She was drawn to this gentle but steady student, who was the first of her pupils to announce himself publicly, in the city directory of Lynn, as a Christian Scientist. Ten years her junior, Asa Eddy and she were married by a Unitarian minister on January 1, 1877. Mary Baker Eddy described the marriage as "a union of affection and . . . high purposes."[8]

Eddy still led the young Christian Science movement, with her husband as her assistant. But the next several years would hand her one challenge after another. As she formed the Christian Scientist Association, the Church of Christ, Scientist, and the Massachusetts Metaphysical College, more problems from past students emerged.

One of Eddy's most successful students, Daniel Spofford, also had hoped to marry her. Instead, he saw many of his patients being

transferred to Asa Eddy after he and Mary married. Spofford agreed instead to spend more time selling and promoting *Science and Health.* Though Asa Eddy did turn his practice back over to Spofford in order to help his wife teach, Spofford left the movement in anger that year when he and Eddy disagreed over publication of the book's next edition. George Barry was another student who had been devoted to Mary, calling her "Mother." After her marriage to Asa Eddy, Barry filed suits against her, charging her for his help over the past five years, and Spofford testified at court trials on Barry's behalf.

The year 1878 was also a challenge. The Eddys were financially strapped. One new student, Edward Arens, suggested they turn to the courts to recoup money owed them by former students, and among those named in suits were Richard Kennedy and Daniel Spofford. Then the Christian Science Association, still struggling for respect, filed a lawsuit against Spofford for using what Mary Eddy called "mental malpractice" on an association member. The newspapers criticized the association, calling the incident another chapter of the Salem witchcraft trials that had occurred in Massachusetts two centuries earlier. The judge dismissed the case, noting that he could not force anyone to control their thoughts. Then, toward the end of the year, Asa Eddy and Edward Arens were arrested and jailed for a supposed conspiracy to murder Spofford, though charges were dropped when witnesses admitted to lying.

Asa Gilbert Eddy was first Mary Baker Eddy's student and later became her third husband.

After that year of setbacks, 1879 saw a more positive development as the Christian Science Association grew into the Church of Christ, Scientist, with twenty-six members. Their church services were much the same then as now: silent, individual prayer, followed by the Lord's Prayer and a sermon. Serving as pastor, Eddy began making plans to center the movement in Boston, even as some students continued to act against Eddy's wishes.

Edward Arens, who had established a successful Christian Science healing practice in Boston, began going his own way. He even published his own pamphlet on healing, much of which he took from *Science and Health*. Eddy eventually won a judgment against him, and his pamphlets were destroyed. In 1881, eight students she had considered a loyal part of her group resigned from the church; they claimed they were tired of her sharp rebukes and what they called her "love of money, and the appearance of hypocrisy."[9] Their accusations were quite a blow to Eddy, who had no idea that they were unhappy with her leadership. She and her husband decided to leave Lynn.

Within a few months, in the spring of 1882, the Eddys moved to a four-story building in Boston to establish the Massachusetts Metaphysical College. They had started the school in Lynn but knew it would be more successful in a large city. Mary had received a charter from the Massachusetts state government, and now graduates of her three-week-long classes would receive a degree for their work. Metaphysics, a philosophy that broadly studies the nature of life, was a popular subject in the 1800s. At first the Eddys' classes had only a few students. But with more people exploring different spiritual viewpoints, their school became a success and attracted students from around the country.

Asa Eddy and two other former students did some teaching, but most students wanted to learn directly from Mary Baker Eddy. She also continued to lead the church and direct Christian Science practitioners who were stationed around the country. The church was meeting in one member's home at the time.

But then another setback occurred. Shortly after their move to Boston, Asa Eddy became ill with what doctors said was heart disease. By June, he was dead. Two doctors associated with the Eddys' college said an autopsy showed heart disease, but at a press conference, Mrs. Eddy announced her husband had died of a different cause—malicious animal magnetism. Asa Eddy would have been saved by Christian Science, she said, if it had been used in time. She claimed her husband was the victim of their former student and healer, Edward Arens.

Robert David Thomas, a psychologist and biographer of Mary Baker Eddy, wrote that Eddy was preoccupied with malicious animal magnetism during the 1870s and 1880s. In an 1881 edition of *Science and Health,* she warned readers that mesmerism was an evil that lurked everywhere. She believed it caused whatever trouble arose between students and herself. She even thought that mesmerists had agents whose job was to "watch . . . every movement of Mrs. Eddy and her students." Correspondence between Christian Scientists had to be mailed secretly, because Eddy believed the "U.S. Post Office was so enveloped in mesmerism."[10]

Thomas believed Eddy's concerns about malicious animal magnetism could be attributed to her struggles in the church's early days, "which were particularly trying for Mrs. Eddy and the movement; . . . she was faced with an unsympathetic outside world."[11] When Eddy felt overwhelmed by attacks from critics and problems with

47

A Christian Science church in Denver, Colorado

her students, Thomas speculates that she "feared she might be separated from God," and her resulting behavior took on "characteristics usually associated with paranoia."[12] One of her students, Samuel Bancroft, recalled that "she suffered intensely from a belief that her work was being retarded by some of those with whom she had shared this knowledge of the power of mind over matter." She feared she had "put a dangerous weapon into their hands, which they were using against her and those who were loyal to her."[13]

By the late 1880s, having continued to lead the growing movement without her husband, Eddy had toned down references to mesmerism, though she still considered it a danger to her movement. In addition to teaching, she spent much of her time defending Christian Science in the church's first regular publication, the *Christian Science Journal*. The movement was spreading west, to new communities like Denver and San Francisco, where new ideas were more welcome. As Christian Science won converts, ministers in other churches warned their congregations about the danger of getting involved with it.

As the church became established, even those critics who did not accept Eddy's teachings must have wondered at the healings that continued to take place. Eddy and her followers boldly called their religion the Truth, and "many of these converts felt they owed Eddy their lives and the meaning they found in living," wrote Stephen Gottschalk, a Christian Scientist.[14] To many of her students, Eddy's teachings represented the Second Coming of Jesus Christ, as mentioned in the Gospel of John in the Bible; another follower even considered her to be a woman mentioned in the Book of Revelations, also written by John. Eddy herself wrote in the *Christian Science Journal* in 1884 that when enough people took her religion to heart, "this attitude of Christ shall once again be in the hearts of his followers," and the Second Coming would be complete.[15] She always stressed that she considered her teachings to be completely Christian.

Eddy spent an enormous amount of time writing encouraging advice to her practitioners in the field, even as these controversies went on. One of the most successful practitioners and lecturers working for her around 1880 was Clara Choate. In a letter, Eddy encouraged her to "be honest, speak the Truth, tell things as they are or not tell them, we must be unselfish and not envious. . . . May God help and bless my dear student, is my constant prayer, and teach and lead her up higher."[16]

Eddy's writings were an important way of establishing the ideas of the church. Eddy started the *Christian Science Journal* in 1883 as a way to reach more of the public. She also added her *Key to the Scriptures*, a glossary of biblical terms and her interpretation of them, to a new edition of *Science and Health*.

In 1885, the church was being criticized by the leading ministers of the day during a popular series of noontime Monday lectures in Boston's Tremont Temple. To many, Eddy's ideas were considered blasphemy, and the London *Times* had reported that American ministers regarded Christian Science as a "dangerous innovation."[17] Others were also using the term "Christian Science" to describe other kinds of religious philosophies. But Eddy was given ten minutes during the lecture series to respond to criticism the church had received, and she used the opportunity to tell the audience of two thousand people that true Christian Science was based on the Bible and wasn't just the latest trend in mental healing.

Being the only teacher at the Massachusetts Metaphysical

College, Eddy had largely given up healing, but she was teaching others the practice. She also trained students to become Christian Science teachers, so they could take the movement to other places in the country. The class to become a teacher cost $100, and would-be practitioners paid $300 to learn healing—large sums of money in the 1880s. But Eddy also offered to teach clergymen for free, and husbands and wives together paid the same as one student.

Eddy's classes were very popular. One student of a class Eddy taught in Chicago wrote, "This grows more glorious every day. . . . It seems to me now as though I was blind before. . . . This Science makes God and the Bible a reality."[18] Becoming a Christian Science practitioner early in the movement often meant financial struggle, but it could also bring personal encouragement from Eddy and eventual success. Classes that once taught only four or five students might now hold twenty. By 1889, Eddy was teaching classes of almost seventy students.

That year, at the height of her movement's success, she stunned Christian Scientists, who now reached into Canada as well as across the United States, with the news that she was shutting down her college. She was tired of fighting within the Christian Science ranks and, as she wrote to a student, tired of teaching. More important, she wanted to devote exclusive time to another revision of *Science and Health*. She resigned as pastor of the church in Boston, dismantled the Christian Science Association and church, and moved to the quiet countryside near Concord, New Hampshire, not far from her childhood home of Bow. From there she would rebuild her movement to prepare it for the day that it would have to continue without her.

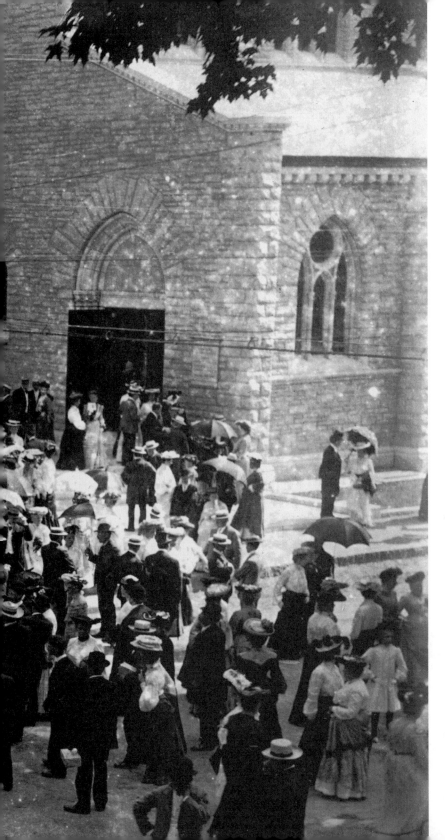

By the end of the nineteenth century, the Church of Christ, Scientist had thousands of members, though Mrs. Eddy prohibited releasing church membership figures. This Christian Science gathering was in Concord, New Hampshire.

WHAT'S IN MARY BAKER EDDY'S BOOK?

Christian Science is based on the words and works of Christ. Mary Baker Eddy's book *Science and Health with Key to the Scriptures* sets forth her teachings so that students can learn the connection between Christ's life and works and the nature of the divine Spirit.

The Church of Christ, Scientist, in its continuing effort to make these teachings readily available, published an edition of *Science and Health* in 1994 that is carried in bookstores and that can be found in libraries.

The Preface introduces the reader to the nature of Spirit, matter, sickness, and the divine Principle.

> Theology and physics teach that both Spirit and matter are real and good, whereas the fact is that Spirit is good and real, and matter is Spirit's opposite. . . . Sickness has been combated for centuries by doctors using material remedies; but the question arises, Is there less sickness because of these practitioners? A vigorous "No" is the response." (p. viii).

> The physical healing of Christian Science results now, as in Jesus' time, from the operation of divine Principle, before which sin and disease lose their reality in human consciousness and disappear as naturally and as necessarily as darkness gives place to light and sin to reformation. Now, as then, these mighty works are not supernatural, but supremely natural. (p. xi)

Chapter 1 describes prayer, the means of Christian Science healing. More generally, prayer is the means of expressing "God's allness"—an understanding that all individuals are children of God, and as His reflections, or expressions, they are always under His care.

> The prayer that reforms the sinner and heals the sick is an absolute faith that all things are possible to God (p. 1) . . . nor can the infinite do less than bestow all good, since He is unchanging wisdom and Love. (p. 2)

> We plead for unmerited pardon and for a liberal outpouring of benefactions. Are we really grateful for the good already received? Then we shall avail ourselves of the blessings we have, and thus be fitted to receive more. (p. 3)

> The habitual struggle to be always good is unceasing prayer. (p. 4)

> In order to pray aright, we must enter into the closet and shut the door. We must close the lips and silence the material senses. In the quiet sanctuary of earnest longings, we must deny sin and plead God's allness. (p. 15)

According to Christian Science doctrine, God's nature—ever-present and wholly good—is seen in the Bible through synonymous names that are either stated or implied, such as divine Mind, Spirit, Soul, Principle, Life, Truth, and Love. Christ, as the mediator between God and humans, is the means for people to recognize the divine Principle that is God.

> He [Jesus] did life's work aright not only in justice to himself, but in mercy to mortals, to show them how to do theirs, but not to do it for them. (p. 18)

Jesus presented the ideal of God better than could any man whose origin was less spiritual. (p. 25)

Our Eucharist is spiritual communion with the one God. (p. 35)

Those who cannot demonstrate, at least in part, the divine Principle of the teachings and practice of our Master [Jesus] have no part in God. (p. 19)

[I]t is the duty and privilege of every child, man, and woman, to follow in some degree the example of the Master by the demonstration of Truth and Life, of health and holiness. (p. 37)

The practice of healing, as Christ and others in the early Christian church performed it, is a means of expressing this connection to God's power and omnipresence. This is the same divine Science that Eddy describes.

[I]n the Christian Church this demonstration of healing was early lost, about 3 centuries after the crucifixion. (p. 41)

In the words of St. John: "He shall give you another Comforter, that he may abide with you forever." This Comforter I understand to be Divine Science. (p. 55)

Anciently the followers of Christ, or Truth, measured Christianity by its power over sickness, sin, and death. (p. 142)

The ancient Christians were healers. Why has this element of Christianity been lost? (p. 146)

In Chapter 6, Eddy notes that the healings that Christ performed were acts performed on mortal bodies, but that they were an expression of the Spiritual. To conduct Christian

Science healing, then, the practitioner must have an understanding of the "supremely natural" divine Principle. This emphasizes the triumph of Spirit over matter.

> I learned these truths in divine Science: that all real being is in God, the divine Mind, and that Life, Truth, and Love are all-powerful and ever-present; that the opposite of Truth, called error, sin, sickness, disease, death, is the false testimony of false material sense, of mind in matter. (p. 108)

> Jesus demonstrated the power of Christian Science to heal mortal minds and bodies. But this power was lost sight of, and must again be spiritually discerned, taught, and demonstrated according to Christ's command. (p. 110)

> Christian Science is natural, but not physical. (p. 111)

> I submitted my metaphysical system of treating disease to the broadest practical tests. Since then this system has gradually gained ground, and has proved itself, whenever scientifically employed, to be the most effective curative agent in medical practice. . . . There can, therefore, be but one method in [Christian Science] teaching. (p. 112)

> There is no pain in Truth, and no truth in pain; no nerve in Mind, and no mind in nerve; no matter in Mind, and mind in matter; no matter in Life, and no life in matter; no matter in good, and no good in matter. (p. 113)

> God is Divine Principle, Life, Truth, Love, Soul, Spirit, Mind. Man is God's spiritual idea, individual, perfect, eternal. (p. 115)

Eddy notes that the Spirit-based practice of Christian Science healing is indeed the opposite of other popular practices that operate by means of matter.

To . . . consider matter as a power in and of itself, is to leave the creator out of His own universe; while to . . . regard God as the creator of matter, is not only to make Him responsible for all disasters, physical and moral, but to announce Him as their source, thereby making Him guilty of maintaining perpetual misrule. (p. 119)

The author calls sick and sinful humanity mortal mind, meaning by this term the flesh opposed to Spirit. . . . [As] the phrase is used in teaching Christian Science, it is meant to designate that which has no real existence. (p. 114)

Worshipping through the medium of matter is paganism. Judaic and other rituals are but types and shadows of true worship. (p. 140)

Understanding the distinction between matter and Spirit explains not only how human ailments can be overcome but how Christ performed miracles. In this same way, people can attain goodness and perfection through study, prayer, and applying spiritual understanding to the overcoming of human afflictions.

The flesh and Spirit can no more unite in action, than good can coincide with evil. (p. 167)

It is profane to fancy that the perfume of clover and the breath of new-mown hay can cause glandular inflammation, sneezing, and nasal pangs. (p. 175)

Human mind produces what is termed organic disease as certainly as it produces hysteria. Mortal mind and body are one.

Neither exists without the other, and both must be destroyed by immortal mind. (p. 177)

Jesus walked on the waves, fed the multitude, healed the sick, and raised the dead in direct opposition to material laws. His acts were the demonstration of Science, overcoming the false claims of material sense or law. (p. 273)

When man demonstrates Christian Science absolutely, he will be perfect. He can neither sin, suffer, be subject to matter, nor disobey the law of God. (p. 372)

From Chapter 14 of *Science and Health*, "Recapitulation":

Jesus beheld in Science the perfect man, who appeared to him where sinning mortal man appears to mortals. In this perfect man the Saviour saw God's own likeness, and this correct view of man healed the sick. (p. 476)

THE CHURCH IN THE MODERN WORLD

5

For twenty years, Mary Baker Eddy had labored not just to bring her vision to the world, but to have at least a part of the world appreciate it as the Truth. The church had fewer than fifty members in 1880, but by 1889, it had grown tremendously. Still, there was much work to be done.

Many people continued to be confused about the church's mission. Other movements, such as one labeled New Thought, borrowed the term "Christian Science" for some of their philosophies or publications, although they had no connection to Eddy's church. Some New Thought members and former Christian Scientists accused her of getting all of her ideas from Phineas Quimby, although it had been twenty years since she had worked with him.

Another problem in understanding the church's goals was that, as Eddy and Christian Science grew more famous, new students wanted to work only with her, and some even considered her divine. She withdrew from public life and broke down the organization in

1889, not to desert it but to strengthen it. Her new revision of *Science and Health* was its fiftieth edition! She wanted to establish the book itself as the teacher of Christian Science.

The branches of the Church of Christ, Scientist that had formed around the country were still operating during Eddy's absence, and she continued to write to her former students about continuing the movement. When she finished revising *Science and Health* in 1891, she prepared, reluctantly, to leave behind her quiet, small-town existence in New Hampshire. She returned to Boston, ready to make that city the base of the Christian Science movement.

The noise of the city was too distracting, Eddy soon discovered, and she went back to New Hampshire, where she would stay for another seventeen years. She bought a farmhouse estate in the country and named it Pleasant View. One view she enjoyed from her new home was of the distant hills near her childhood home of Bow. Though she was seventy years old, she was nowhere near retiring. The first phase of her Christian Science movement had been completed. Now she was ready to tackle the next phase.

Eddy so far had avoided putting much structure into her church movement. She thought church rituals made too much use of the world of matter, or error. Christian Science's lack of rituals caused people to focus instead on individual commitment to God. In this way, it recalled the Puritan faith Eddy had grown up with. The church she created has no sacraments to celebrate, such as baptism or confirmation. It has no ordained clergy; in fact, marriage ceremonies must be performed by ministers of other Christian denominations.

But Eddy realized the church needed at least some structure. She and twelve other Christian Scientists established "The Mother

Mary Baker Eddy became much less active in public life when she moved from Boston to Pleasant View, her spacious home in the New Hampshire countryside near Concord. Sometimes she addressed her followers from the balcony of the house.

Church," The First Church of Christ, Scientist, in Boston in 1892. A church building in Boston was completed in 1894, the construction of which was overseen by the church's board of directors. Eddy published *The Manual of The Mother Church,* which still governs it today and which, like *Science and Health,* is considered divinely

The First Church of Christ, Scientist, or Mother Church, was completed in 1894 (right) in Boston. It outgrew its seating of 1,100 within a few years, and an extension (left) was added in 1906.

inspired. The Mother Church is a central authority, but each branch church governs itself. Members of branch churches can become members of the Mother Church as well as their own. Eddy ran the church movement from Pleasant View while she wrote articles for the *Christian Science Journal* and other booklets. She often had several students staying and working there, and she continued to teach classes on Christian Science in Concord until 1898.

By the 1890s, her church had grown to include thousands of members, and Eddy was famous. Many considered it a great achievement to see her in person, and sometimes people would camp outside her gate just to catch a glimpse of her. One church member claimed to trace Eddy's family roots, like Christ's, back to David in the Bible. But she did not consider herself the equal of Jesus. In her seclusion, the more her church grew, the more she became a curiosity figure to church members and non-Christian Scientists alike.

Some Christian Scientists, who were more concerned with their own power than with the Christian worship of God, publicized other events. A church leader named Josephine Woodbury, for example, gave birth to a son in 1890, though she hadn't had marital relations with her husband for several years. She declared it to be a virgin birth, much like that of Jesus' mother, Mary, and she baptized her son "The Prince of Peace." She was excommunicated from the church a few years later. Embarrassing situations like that were helped when the Mother Church formed a Board of Lectureship to spread the Christian Science word among the public. A weekly publication, the *Christian Science Sentinel*, started in the 1890s to aid this effort.

The regular practices of Christian Scientists were not so very mysterious. By 1895, their church services were much as they are today: "readers," rather than preachers, are chosen by the congregation within each church to read passages from *Science and Health* and the Bible. They conduct Wednesday evening prayer services that include testimonials of Christian Science healing. In this quiet way, the church continued to attract new members in the late 1800s. The Mother Church in Boston, with seating for 1,100, was not big enough; in 1906, a huge addition was completed. By this time, the

Samuel Clemens, who wrote books such as Huckleberry Finn *under the name of Mark Twain, was a frequent and outspoken critic of Christian Science and especially Mary Baker Eddy.*

church had spread to Europe as well. It wasn't surprising, then, to hear Eddy predict that the church would "be the dominant religious belief of the world" in another fifty years.

The most famous critic of Christian Science in Mary Baker Eddy's day was the writer Samuel Clemens, known as Mark Twain. He thought Eddy had a tight ruling grip on church members. (She did claim to be infallible, or always correct, as leader of her church.) He also thought she made too much money and spent too much on beautiful church buildings rather than on charitable causes, such as "orphans, widows, discharged prisoners, hospitals, . . . missions, libraries, old peoples' homes."[1] But at the same time, he couldn't help but call Eddy "the most interesting woman who ever lived."[2]

Eddy replied to critics like Mark Twain by reminding them of the life- and soul-saving healing work Christian Scientists performed. The Church of Christ, Scientist, then, as now, considers prayer an important contribution to the world; for example, Eddy asked Christian Scientists to pray daily to end the war between Russia and Japan early in the 1900s. Christian Scientists as individuals often answer Jesus' call to serve others, and churches may offer help during disasters such as earthquakes or floods, but the churches as a whole seldom participate in ongoing social outreach programs, such as soup kitchens or other ministries. In general, Christian Science reading rooms and free lectures are the main ways for churches to interact with their communities.

Another way for the church to communicate with the world was through the establishment of a daily Christian Science newspaper, the *Christian Science Monitor,* in 1908. Eddy considered this paper and *Science and Health* her greatest accomplishments. Ironically, she

The *Christian Science Monitor* is almost ninety years old and has been through many changes since it first came off the presses in 1908. The Church of Christ, Scientist subsidizes (provides financial support for) the paper, seeing it as a public service. But the paper is not just a mouthpiece for its parent organization; it is a highly respected news source with a reputation for thorough analysis of the stories of the day.

The newspaper grew out of Mary Baker Eddy's lifelong interest in the world around her, an interest that grew as she aged. For Christian Scientists, the *Monitor* was to serve as an educational tool, making them aware of where their prayers might be especially needed. For all newspaper readers, it offered an alternative to the "muckraking" dailies that competed for readers' attention with sensational stories.

Today, a quick read of the *Monitor* may not reveal many differences from other daily newspapers. It contains national and international news, sports and feature stories, and an editorial page. The only clue that it is associated with a church (besides the name of the newspaper, of course!) is the daily "Religious Article" that appears in the editorial pages.

The real difference between the *Christian Science Monitor* and other daily newspapers is more subtle. It doesn't ignore the troublesome news around the world or in the United States, but the *Monitor* presents that news in a different light.

Coverage in the *Monitor* of the April 1995 bombing of the Alfred Murrah federal building in Oklahoma City provides an example of their different approach to events. The *Monitor* gave it much coverage, as other papers were doing, but bad news tended to be balanced with accounts of people doing positive things as a result—donating blood, for example, or sending in money and manpower to help in rescue efforts. An editorial did not cry out for justice or revenge, but instead called for patience and cool heads. The daily "Religious Article" a week later offered the idea that there *is* a place safe from terrorists: "in the realm of Spirit. Terrorism, and the mentality that would mount it, are utterly foreign to God and His Kingdom, His consciousness."

The bad news one reads in most newspapers is presented plainly and starkly, and the individual reader must figure out what it all means by himself or herself. The *Christian Science Monitor* reports the same news, but readers will always find something with that news that suggests reasons for hope and optimism. This attitude is aimed not exclusively toward Christian Scientists—about half of the subscribers to the *Monitor,* in fact, are not Christian Scientists. Mary Baker Eddy's mission of the *Monitor* always was "to injure no man, but to bless all mankind."

started the *Monitor* shortly after a New York newspaper described her as having become senile and physically feeble. It contended that those living with her were keeping her imprisoned in her home while stealing her money. That article caused her son, George, and another son she had adopted in 1888 to file suit to take charge of her affairs; they declared her incompetent to do so. She was eighty-six years old in 1907, when a psychiatrist who interviewed her for the trial told the *New York Times,* "For a woman of her age I do not hesitate to say that she is physically and mentally phenomenal." She defeated the lawsuit, and the next year she started the newspaper, motivated partly by the less-than-truthful stories that appeared in other influential newspapers.

Eddy had always been interested in public affairs. She wanted Christian Scientists to get a realistic, but not pessimistic, view of their country and the world to give them a good idea of where their prayers might be especially needed. She formed the idea in August 1908 and presented it to the church Board of Directors and the Mother Church's Board of Trustees, and the first issue of the *Christian Science Monitor* was on newsstands by Thanksgiving. "The object of the *Monitor* is to injure no man, but to bless all mankind," she wrote in the first issue's editorial. She called on Christian Scientists to read it and subscribe to it. Over the years, the *Monitor* has grown to be considered a top American newspaper.

Living near Boston once again, Eddy continued to direct the church in 1909 and into 1910. She set aside a part of each day for a carriage ride, as she'd done for years. She had gone through some painful illnesses in her later years, including kidney stones; doctors were consulted, and she even received pain medication toward the

Up to the end of her life, Mrs. Eddy enjoyed daily carriage rides, one of the few chances that the public had to see her.

end of her life. She died on December 3, 1910, leaving behind a thriving movement.

Obituaries across the country noted her impact on all of American society. In Massachusetts, the *Springfield Union* noted, "About no personage of her generation has so much and such bitter controversy raged as around the Founder and Leader of . . . Christian Science." The *Chicago Tribune* commented that at her death "there passes from this world's activities one of the most remarkable women of her time."

Some wondered if the Church of Christ, Scientist would survive without the strong presence of its founder. Mary Baker Eddy spent the last part of her life making sure it would.

THE CHURCH AFTER MARY BAKER EDDY

6

When Mary Baker Eddy died, the question of leading her church was supposed to be a non-issue: she left her writings, *The Manual of The Mother Church* and *Science and Health with Key to the Scriptures,* to direct her followers, along with the Bible. She even planned the twenty-six topics of discussions and accompanying Bible and *Science and Health* passages for reading in the Sunday church services. They are still used today and repeated in full twice each year.

But leadership of the church became a very difficult issue. One member, Augusta Stetson, tried to become head of the entire church, and she hinted that she was using malicious animal magnetism on those who were near Eddy shortly before her death. One of Stetson's targets, Archibald McLellan, said he survived the "mental attack," and he led the five-member church board of directors after Eddy's death.

The Church of Christ, Scientist was enjoying good financial

Archibald McLellan ran the Christian Science church board of directors after the death of Mrs. Eddy in 1910. The early church's members were mostly poor factory workers, but by the twentieth century, many prominent members, such as McLellan, were from prominent American and European society.

times. Its members were generous, raising money for mortgage-free churches often in the best neighborhoods of cities such as New York and London. In her will, Eddy left several million dollars as a trust fund for the church, and sale of her books continued to generate income for the Mother Church. In 1906, the Christian Scientists had 638 churches and societies, and by 1912 that number had more than doubled. In fact, it was the fastest growing church in the country. Shortly after Eddy's death, worldwide membership was estimated to be as high as 150,000.

One unique aspect of Christian Science was its much higher number of women in the church than men; even Eddy had mentioned the need for more male church members. Among Christian Scientist practitioners, women outnumbered men as much as eight to one in the early 1970s. An article in the *Christian Science Journal* in 1895 said the church gave women opportunities to work in "the two noblest of all avocations, philanthropy and medicine," and "placed women by the side of men in the pulpit." Women were attracted to the church in part because Mary Baker Eddy was a supporter of women's issues such as the right to vote. Even so, men have usually held the most influential positions in the church, such as heads of the Publications Society or Board of Directors.

In 1950, a *Time* magazine article noted that things kept getting "better and better" for the church. In the 1960s and 1970s, Christian Scientists served in high government positions, such as judges, the heads of the Federal Bureau of Investigators and the Central Intelligence Agency, and as prominent White House aides for Richard Nixon.

But by the end of the 1970s, "better and better" no longer described the situation of the Church of Christ, Scientist. Membership figures were down, dozens of churches closed during that decade, and the number of Christian Science practitioners had fallen off rapidly. In 1979, the Christian Science church was free of debt and had about 70 million dollars cash on hand. In the *Wall*

Street Journal, writer Robert Peel described the decline in membership as a "pause, a chance for second wind." But the membership situation was a big enough concern to the church board of directors, according to church insiders like Stephen Gottschalk, that they gambled on a plan to win new members. The *Christian Science Monitor*

had brought the church respect over the years; perhaps the appeal of its style of journalism could be expanded to another medium—television. But within ten years the church had lost more than 300 million dollars, as attempts to start up a 24-hour cable news station, called the Monitor Channel, were struggling.

Another financial controversy, in the form of a forty-three-year-old book, arose in 1993. The book, called *The Destiny of the Mother Church*, had been privately published by Christian Science teacher Bliss Knapp who, as a child, had met Mary Baker Eddy. Knapp's parents were devout Christian Scientists in Eddy's day. Bliss Knapp taught and lectured on Christian Science; he began telling students that a woman mentioned in the Book of Revelations in the Bible's New Testament was none other than Mary Baker Eddy. In 1947, he published *The Destiny of the Mother Church*, which was a mixture of his own family history, some history of Mary Baker Eddy, and his own views on Christian Science, which included the exaltation of Eddy as the equal of Jesus Christ. He hoped the church would promote the book and carry it in its reading rooms. Not only did the church reject it, but the board of directors asked him to get back the copy he had sent to the Library of Congress and destroy it as well as the plates from which the book had been printed.

Forty years later, the book became more appealing to church leaders; Knapp, who had married into a wealthy family and died in 1958, willed the church more than 90 million dollars on the condition that his book be published by 1993 and sold by the church as official Christian Science literature. In 1991, the church did just that, only to find itself the target of church members' protests. One Christian Science teacher was quoted in the magazine *Christian Century* in November 1991 as saying, "Members who are actually reading the book are finding its viewpoint preposterous and outrageous." Eddy herself often warned church members not to consider her divine; she stated this order in *The Manual of The Mother Church*, which the board of directors is obligated to follow.

As church members became more aware of the money their church had spent on the Monitor Channel and of the publication of a book that, many believed, went against official church doctrine, they insisted the board of directors act more cautiously. In 1992, Church of Christ, Scientist Board of Directors chairman Harvey Wood stepped down, replaced by Virginia S. Harris, and the Monitor Channel was put up for sale.

As the church struggled with finances and doctrine, another issue had also been emerging, this one much more publicly. In the 1980s, in areas as varied as Arizona, California, Minnesota, and Massachusetts, Christian Science parents were being prosecuted for the deaths of their sick children. The broad issue is the right of Christian Science parents to practice their religious beliefs, versus the obligation of the state to protect children from harm. Some former Christian Scientists, however, felt the laws should do more to ensure a child's right to live.

One woman who grew up in a Christian Science home, Caroline Fraser, wrote an article in *Atlantic Monthly* magazine in April 1995 criticizing the church attitude toward seriously ill children: "Imagine being told by their parents that their illness is not real and that the pain they feel is not a part of the real world—God's world." In one well-publicized case, a twelve-year-old girl had a leg tumor that grew to the size of a large watermelon; she died in June 1988 at a Christian Science nursing home, eight months after leaving school. The girl's parents were indicted on child-abuse charges

Most Christian Science parents choose not to have their children immunized to prevent disease. Instead, they rely on an understanding of God as gained through their study of the Bible and Mrs. Eddy's writings. Illness, Mrs. Eddy wrote, is not real, but only seems real.

and a year later pleaded guilty to reckless endangerment, a misdemeanor in their state.

Other parents have also been prosecuted on charges of neglect. The exact number is hard to determine. Cited in the *Atlantic Monthly* magazine article is the research of former Christian Scientist

Rita Swan. She discovered from coroners' and other records "at least 165 children who have died since 1975 because medical care was withheld for religious reasons," but not all of those children were from Christian Science families.

Fraser and others note ways in which Christian Science healing can be one aspect of treating the sick in today's high-technology world. Fraser wrote of Suzanne Shepard, a former Christian Science practitioner who took her daughter to a hospital when the child slipped into a coma from a ruptured appendix. Shepard's belief was "that prayer could be combined with medicine." Mary Baker Eddy herself made use of doctors and pain killers in her old age, and Christian Scientists receive treatment such as exams from eye doctors and dentists.

For devout Christian Scientists, it is considered unfaithful to expect "matter," such as drugs, to get rid of "error," or sickness. Their faith in spiritual healing is based on positive experiences with the practice. *Science and Health* describes the basis of healing by saying, "Spirit is good and real, and matter is Spirit's opposite."[1] It addresses medicine more directly, too: "If He creates drugs at all and designs them for medical use, why did Jesus not employ them and recommend them for the treatment of disease?"[2] The sorrow devout Christian Science parents would naturally feel after a child's death can be compounded by what they see as their failure to heal with Science, but not as the failure of Science itself. One Massachusetts father, whose two-year-old son died from a medically-treatable bowel obstruction, said, "If we were closer to God we could have stopped this from happening. In that way I blame myself."

Laws in Great Britain and Germany, where many of the world's Christian Scientists live, prevent parents from making that choice:

medical treatment for seriously ill children is required of all parents, regardless of religion. In the United States, the church hopes Christian Science parents will realize they have what it sees as a valuable right in the United States—the right to rely solely on divine Science for healing. The controversy has focused on certain publicized events. The practice itself is much more prevalent, and in fact is just one aspect of the Christian Scientists' belief system. As one church member noted, "Christian Science has been healing children of all kinds of illnesses—in many cases those given up by the medical profession—for 130 years."[3]

THE SCOPE OF CHRISTIAN SCIENCE HEALING 7

Headlines in American newspapers from coast to coast have reported the sad news of the deaths of children when Christian Science healing did not save their lives. But as Stephen Gottschalk noted, "It is ironic that Christian Science healing should be attracting attention more by its failure than by its successes."[1] A look at Christian Science healing helps in understanding how their doctrine works in other areas of life as well.

Those successes have occurred by the thousands, according to testimonies given orally or in writing since the days when the church began keeping track of them. Mary Baker Eddy included one hundred pages of healing incidents in *Science and Health,* in a section called "Fruitage." The weekly *Christian Science Sentinel* has been including accounts of healing since it first appeared more than a hundred years ago, and books such as *Healing Spiritually,* published by the church, and *Spiritual Healing in a Scientific Age* by Robert Peel, offer many more examples. For a Christian Science

Devout Christian Science parents rely on their faith alone for almost all aspects of healing for themselves and their children. The parents of this three-year-old boy, who according to X rays had a fractured skull, refused medical treatment for their son, instead relying on Christian Science treatment. Eleven days after his accident, the boy was back outside playing.

healing testimony to be considered valid, it must be verified by three other church members who are familiar with the incident or who know the person giving the testimony. Sometimes, medical reports, such as X rays or a written diagnosis by a doctor, accompany the testimonies.

One member of the church explained that his decision to rely on Christian Science for healing came from his own experience with it. It is not just blind faith that causes people to turn to spiritual healing. Rather, their past positive experiences with healing demonstrate its effectiveness, he said. He compared sin and sickness to "waking nightmares, from which we must awaken."[2] How does one accomplish that? Following are some "awakening" accounts of other Christian Scientists, from the early days of the church to the present.

Some healings have been achieved just by reading *Science and Health*. In the book's "Fruitage" section are accounts like the following: A man in Salt Lake City, Utah, was riding his bike home for lunch one day when he fell off, landing "on my left side with my arm under my head." He felt sure he had broken his upper arm. He managed to get home; then he asked his young son to find their copy of *Science and Health,* "which I read for about ten minutes, when all pain left."

He did not say anything about the accident to his family: "My friends claimed that the arm had not been broken." One friend suggested he visit a doctor to get another opinion. The doctor examined an X ray of the arm and said, "Yes, it has been broken, but whoever set it made a perfect job of it." The man added, "My friend then asked the doctor to show how he could tell where the break had been. The doctor pointed out the place as being slightly thicker at that part, like a piece of steel that had been welded."[3]

Also from "Fruitage" is this early account: "I was afflicted with a fibroid tumor which weighed not less than fifty pounds, attended by a continuous hemorrhage for eleven years. The tumor was a growth of eighteen years." The testifier moved to Chicago from Texas in 1887, and had never before heard of Christian Science. "After being there several weeks I received letters from a Texas lady who had herself been healed, and who wrote urging me to try Christian Science.

"Changing my boarding-place, I met a lady who owned a copy of *Science and Health,* and . . . she got it and told me I could read it. The revelation was marvelous and brought a great spiritual awakening. This awakened sense never left me, and one day when walking alone it came to me very suddenly that I was healed, and I walked the faster declaring every step that I was healed. When I reached my boarding-place, I found my hostess and told her I was healed. She looked the picture of amazement. The tumor began to disappear at once, the hemorrhage had ceased, and perfect strength was manifest. . . . I must add that the reading of *Science and Health,* and that alone, healed me."[4]

Many healing stories that appear in Christian Science church literature such as the *Sentinel* involve children. Following are two incidents provided as well as verified by the Mother Church's Committee on Publication:

In 1954, during a polio outbreak in her neighborhood, Sheila Norris, age nine, awoke one morning with a fever. She found it impossible to turn or move her head without pain. Because of the proximity of several other polio cases, the family became alarmed.

Sheila's parents asked her what she preferred to do. Sheila remembers her strong support for the family's choice to have her mother call a Christian Science practitioner and not to seek any medical treatment.

For a period of four days, her condition grew steadily more alarming, until she was unable to move her body at all without great pain. On the fifth day, dramatic healing changes took place as her parents prayed earnestly with the Christian Science practitioner. On the sixth day, Sheila was able to get up without pain. She had no more evidence of a fever. On the seventh day, Sheila was well enough to attend a Christian Science Sunday School with only a slight stiffness in her neck.

Although she had lost weight and color during the episode, she returned the following Monday to school with very little evidence of ever having been seriously ill. The healing has remained complete. It was first published in the Christian Science *Sentinel* of October 6, 1956. Almost thirty-eight years later, Sheila Norris Chaps verified the permanency of her healing.

More recently, in Stanton, Kentucky, Charles Southworth went from a few isolated instances of unusual behavior during his junior year in high school to the point where, during the summer before his senior year, he began suffering terribly with epilepsy. At the worst point, he had an average of two to three seizures each day, usually followed by hours of sleep and severe headaches.

With each episode, his parents engaged a Christian Science practitioner, and Charles seemed to respond well to the treatment. When the seizures became more frequent, however, they made an appointment with a neurological specialist. The diagnosis was grand mal epilepsy. The doctor could offer no cure at all. He prescribed

Dilantin to calm the seizures, and he was quite clear about the possible side effects. He said that Charles would have to learn to live with this condition and take this medication for the rest of his life.

Charles chose not to use the drug, and the family never filled the prescription. Instead, they called a Christian Science practitioner again. Within a very short time, the seizures decreased dramatically and, within a couple of months, they stopped altogether. After his high school graduation, Charles was employed as a delivery van driver in Lexington, Kentucky.

Today, Charles is twenty-four years old and regularly drives long distances in a rig for a large trucking company. No signs of epilepsy have ever recurred.

A recent church publication is the 1994 booklet *Addiction Can Be Healed*. In it, a woman writes that when she was a college student, at a late hour one night, she was not allowed to leave her dormitory room to buy cigarettes. As she prayed the Christian Science version of the Lord's Prayer, she felt as though someone was asking her: which was stronger, herself or a cigarette? And who is more powerful, a cigarette or God? She bought more cigarettes in the morning, but she never opened them and never smoked again.

In a 1995 issue of the *Christian Science Sentinel,* a woman wrote that while it might seem ridiculous to some to say disease is not real, such is usually the actual experience of Christian Scientists. She wrote about one of her experiences in particular, in which, despite her prayers, she was bothered by a painful growth on her arm. Her boss at work asked her why she didn't do something about the wart, such as have it surgically removed. She told him she felt committed to the same approach to healing used by Jesus, and she still believed God would heal her.

One evening shortly after her conversation with her boss, she was in her backyard, contemplating the first chapter of Genesis in the Bible, and thinking how pleased God was with his creation, which didn't include disease. Having feared the growth on her arm would be permanent, it then occurred to her that as the child of a loving God who created only goodness, she could be free of imperfections. She concluded that the wart couldn't possibly be a part of her. She knew then she was healed, and within a few days all signs of the growth were gone.

Mary Baker Eddy strongly believed that suffering and sin were a result of misunderstanding God, so Christian Scientists are encouraged to pray and read the Bible and *Science and Health* every day. Daily prayer and study reinforce Christian Science teachings. By studying true spiritual nature, one moves closer to truly understanding God. The practice of healing is one part of this meditation and study. By relying on God for healing instead of medicine, Christian Scientists are spending more time in prayer than they would if medicine were used instead.

Some of the most remarkable healings in Christian Science were performed by Mrs. Eddy. For example, she became reacquainted with her adult son George, who was living in Deadwood in the Dakota Territory (now South Dakota), when he visited her in Massachusetts in 1879. Robert Peel writes in his biography of Mrs. Eddy, "While in Boston he [George] had mentioned to Mrs. Eddy that his three-year-old daughter, Mary Baker Glover, was cross-eyed, and Mrs. Eddy's quiet response had been, 'You must be mistaken, George; her eyes are all right.' On returning to Deadwood he found that they were indeed all right."[5]

Electa Bessler, an investment broker who lives in Indiana,

believes she was healed of what may have been a broken rib. She recalled that one Saturday afternoon in 1994, "I was in a serious auto accident, when a semi [tractor-trailer truck] ran into me and pushed me into a bridge retaining wall." Though she suspected broken or at least badly bruised ribs, when police arrived, she refused to be brought to an emergency room, where an X ray would have been taken and medical treatment conducted. Instead, she called her husband, who is not a Christian Scientist.

"Initially, there was a lot of fear," she said, of having long-lasting injuries. "I just stayed very close in prayer," with the help of a practitioner, to the idea that "I could not be outside of God's tender care." As she recuperated, she overcame her fear by thinking that "God is good and ever present. Evil could not be real for me, or anywhere else." Finally, as she was expressing gratitude for God's perfection, and "claiming my place in that perfection," she noticed all fear had left her. "Usually when the fear is gone, healing comes." She returned to work part-time the Wednesday after her accident and full-time the Monday after that.[6]

ON BEING A CHRISTIAN SCIENTIST TODAY

8

The big window of the main Christian Science Reading Room in Cincinnati, Ohio, looks out onto a busy downtown street. It offers a perfect view of the kind of people who might stop in there on any given day: professional men and women in business suits, or older pedestrians who aren't in such a hurry. Then there are those with emotional or drinking problems who get little eye contact from the other pedestrians. But they can always count on a friendly welcome from someone in the reading room. It is there for everyone.

Deb Simons, who recently became a Christian Science practitioner and also helps out in the reading room, said the amount of activity and the types of visitors there vary. Lots of people stop by out of curiosity. Recently, a retired Russian doctor came in, "very interested in the idea of healing without medicine," said Ms. Simons. "We offered him some literature." People coming in often want Bibles or children's nondenominational books, such as Bible stories.

Sometimes people come in worried over a situation in their lives and want someone to pray with them, another kind of service they can find at a reading room. If a person is seeking help for alcoholism, for example, the reading room attendant is likely to try and offer comfort as well as reassurance "that they are God's child, that they are loved, and that prayer does help. It doesn't matter what they've done, because every day is a fresh start," Ms. Simons said. "We try not to preach to people, but we aren't bashful about offering *Science and Health*."

On the outside door facing the sidewalk is a box with free literature such as the *Christian Science Sentinel* and other booklets. One of the most popular items given away, said Ms. Simons, is the church's *Quarterly Bible Lesson*. It contains excerpts from the Bible and from *Science and Health* that Christian Scientists will hear read at their upcoming Sunday church service. All of the Bible and *Science and Health* readings that Christian Scientists hear each week were put together by Mary Baker Eddy before her death. She wanted to replace preaching, which can vary in effectiveness from one person to another, with Scripture reading; *Science and Health* is included in that category, because Christian Scientists consider it divinely inspired.

But not everyone whom the Christian Science church wants to

The world headquarters of the Church of Christ, Scientist, a landmark in Boston, includes the Mother Church, a 700-foot-long reflecting pool, and a twenty-six-story administration building at one end of the pool.

reach happens to walk by a reading room. So church members distribute and leave church literature such as the *Sentinel,* as well as the *Christian Science Monitor,* in public places like Laundromats, bus stations, and even hospitals, when they are permitted to do so.

Deb Simons came to Christian Science when pregnant with her first child. Her blood pressure was dangerously high, but after praying with a Christian Scientist friend it became normal, and her delivery was normal, too. "It was like someone had opened the door of a whole new world that I hadn't known existed," she said. She raised her three children "in Science," and all of them have stayed with it, "because they really saw it work" as they grew.

In addition to keeping up with the church's *Bible Lessons,* personal prayer is also a significant part of a faithful Christian Scientist's daily life. Adults and children try to protect themselves through prayer from mortal mind which, they believe, lets into the human consciousness false beliefs about illness, accidents, or other events in life that can cause us to be afraid. Such beliefs, it is thought, are what separate us from God's spiritual and perfect world.

For Christian Scientists, every aspect of life is connected to the striving for perfection. Some Christian Scientists believe the church's declining membership figures from the last few decades stem from a society that is not able to commit itself to the radical lifestyle changes the church encourages: no drinking of alcohol or caffeine, no smoking, no premarital sex, and an honest attempt at being totally reliant on God for all aspects of physical and emotional well-being.

Church outreach will continue to consist of reading rooms and lectures open to the public, as well as the *Christian Science Monitor.* Christian Science radio programs air daily on shortwave radio, and videos of the church's daily lessons from the Bible and *Science and Health* are available to television stations throughout the country for public service programming.

The Mother Church has been trying to make the public more aware of the writings of Mary Baker Eddy, and sales of *Science and Health* have increased in the past few years in retail bookstores. The Mother Church is also trying to increase the readership of the *Christian Science Monitor*. Another effective way to gather in new members would be "more good healing," said Deb Simons. The church is growing in the continent of Africa, as well as in pockets of America where it hadn't existed before. *Science and Health* continues to reach out to new audiences. And church members continue in their quest for perfection, through prayer.

SOURCE NOTES

Chapter One

1. Gottschalk, Stephen, *The Emergence of Christian Science in American Religious Life* (Berkeley: University of California Press, 1973), p. 197.

Chapter Two

1. Peel, Robert, *Christian Science: Its Encounter with American Culture* (New York: Henry Holt and Co., 1958), p. 7.
2. Ramsey, E. Mary, *Christian Science and Its Discoverer* (Boston: The Christian Science Publishing Society, 1935), p. 24.
3. Thomas, Robert David, *"With Bleeding Footsteps": Mary Baker Eddy's Path to Religious Leadership* (New York: Alfred A. Knopf, 1994), pp. 87–89.
4. Thomas, p. 102.

Chapter Three

1. Thomas, Robert David, *"With Bleeding Footsteps": Mary Baker Eddy's Path to Religious Leadership* (New York: Alfred A. Knopf, 1994), p. 117.
2. Ramsey, E. Mary, *Christian Science and Its Discoverer* (Boston: The Christian Science Publishing Society, 1935), p. 63.
3. Thomas, p. 131.
4. Peel, Robert, *Mary Baker Eddy: The Years of Trial* (Boston: The Christian Science Publishing Society, 1971), pp. 20–21.
5. Thomas, p. 146.
6. Ramsey, p. 74.

Chapter Four

1. Peel, Robert, *Mary Baker Eddy: The Years of Trial* (Boston: The Christian Science Publishing Society, 1971), p. 14.
2. Gottschalk, Stephen, *The Emergence of Christian Science in American Religious Life* (Berkeley: University of California Press, 1973), p. 36.
3. Eddy, Mary Baker, *Science and Health with Key to the Scriptures* (Boston: The First Church of Christ, Scientist, 1994), p. 581.
4. Eddy, p. 40.
5. Eddy, p. 589.
6. Eddy, p. 266.
7. Ibid.
8. Thomas, Robert David, *"With Bleeding Footsteps": Mary Baker Eddy's Path to Religious Leadership* (New York: Alfred A. Knopf, 1994), p. 152.

9. Thomas, p. 155.

10. Thomas, p. 163.

11. Thomas, p. 167.

12. Ibid.

13. Peel, *Mary Baker Eddy: The Years of Trial,* p. 36.

14. Gottschalk, p. xviii.

15. Gottschalk, p. xxi.

16. Peel, *Mary Baker Eddy: The Years of Trial,* p. 80.

17. Gottschalk, p. xvii.

18. Peel, *Mary Baker Eddy: The Years of Trial,* p. 161.

Chapter Five

1. Gottschalk, Stephen, *The Emergence of Christian Science in American Religious Life* (Berkeley: University of California Press, 1973), p. 270.

2. Peel, Robert, *Christian Science: Its Encounter with American Culture* (New York: Henry Holt and Co., 1958), p. 167.

Chapter Six

1. Eddy, Mary Baker, *Science and Health with Key to the Scriptures* (Boston: The First Church of Christ, Scientist, 1994), p. viii.

2. Eddy, p. 157.

3. Letter to author.

Chapter Seven

1. *Christian Century,* June 22–29, 1988.

2. As told to author.

3. Eddy, Mary Baker, *Science and Health with Key to the Scrip-*

tures (Boston: The First Church of Christ, Scientist, 1994), pp. 605–607.

4. Eddy, p. 603.

5. Peel, Robert, *Mary Baker Eddy: The Years of Trial* (Boston: The Christian Science Publishing Society, 1971), p. 71.

6 As told to author.

FOR FURTHER READING

Cather, Willa, and Georgine Milmine. *The Life of Mary Baker G. Eddy & the History of Christian Science*. Lincoln: University of Nebraska Press, 1993. First published in 1909.

A Century of Christian Science Healing. Boston: The Christian Science Publishing Society, 1966.

Eddy, Mary Baker. *Science and Health with Key to the Scriptures: Authorized Edition*. Boston: The First Church of Christ, Scientist, 1994.

Gottschalk, Stephen. *The Emergence of Christian Science in American Religious Life*. Berkeley: University of California Press, 1973.

Knee, Stuart E. *Christian Science in the Age of Mary Baker Eddy*. Contributions in American History Series. Westport, Conn.: Greenwood Press, 1994.

Peel, Robert. *Christian Science: Its Encounter with American Culture*. Harrington Park, N.J.: Robert H. Sommer, 1986. (First published by Henry Holt and Co., New York, 1958.)

Peel, Robert. *Mary Baker Eddy*. 3 Volumes. Boston: The Christian Science Publishing Society, 1966–77.
Volume 1: *The Years of Discovery* (1966).
Volume 2: *The Years of Trial* (1971).
Volume 3: *The Years of Authority* (1977).

Ramsay, E. Mary. *Christian Science and Its Discoverer*. Boston: The Christian Science Publishing Society, 1963. (First published in 1935.)

Thomas, Robert David. *"With Bleeding Footsteps": Mary Baker Eddy's Path to Religious Leadership*. New York: Alfred A. Knopf, 1994.

Twain, Mark (Samuel Clemens). *Christian Science*. Buffalo, N.Y.: Prometheus Books, 1986. (First published in 1907.)

INTERNET SITES

Due to the changeable nature of the Internet, sites appear and disappear very quickly. Internet addresses must be entered with capital and lowercase letters exactly as they appear.

The Yahoo directory of the World Wide Web is an excellent place to find Internet sites on any topic. The directory is located at:

http://www.yahoo.com

The official home page of The Church of Christ, Scientist contains questions and answers about Christian Scientists, information about the Pastor of the Church of Christ, Scientist, information about Mary Baker Eddy, a "visit" to the First Church of Christ, Scientist in Boston, reprints of religion articles from the *Christian Science Monitor*, and more. It is located at:

http://www.tfccs.com

INDEX

ABOUT THE AUTHOR

Jean Kinney Williams grew up in Ohio and lives there now with her husband and four children. She studied journalism in college and, in addition to writing, enjoys reading, volunteering at church, and spending time with her family. She is the author of the Franklin Watts First Book *Matthew Hensen: Polar Adventurer* (1994) and of two other American Religious Experience books, *The Amish* and *The Mormons* (both 1996).